The Color of $ale and Customers

Using your
understanding of
personality types with
prospects and clients

George J. Boelcke, F.C.I.

Also by George Boelcke:

- Colorful Personalities: Discover Your
  Personality Type Through the Power of Colors
- Colorful Personalities: Audio CD
- The Colors of Leadership and Management
- The Colors of Parent and Child Dynamics
- The Colors of Relationships
- Keep Your Money! The insights of credit & debt:
  What you have to know – what you need to avoid
- ¡Quédese con Su Dinero! Los Secretos del Crédito y la Deuda
  Lo que tiene que saber – Lo que necesita evitar
- It's Your Money! Tools, Tips and Tricks
  to Borrow Smarter and Pay It Off Quicker
  US - Spanish & Canadian Editions
  (www.yourmoneybook.com)

To Contact the Author:

George Boelcke facilitates seminars throughout North America for companies and organizations ranging from Fortune 500 firms to small businesses, church groups, relationship seminars, conventions and schools. George can be contacted:

By e-mail: george@vantageseminars.com
Via web-site: www.vantageseminars.com
By mail: U.S.: 1183-14781 Memorial Dr. Houston, TX 77079
        Canada: Box 4080, Edmonton, AB T6E 4S8

Library and Archives Canada Cataloguing in Publication

Boelcke, George J., 1959–
        The colors of sales and customers : using your understanding of
        personality types with prospects & clients / George J. Boelcke. — 2nd ed.

Includes index.
ISBN 0-9736668-6-2

        1. Selling—Psychological aspects. 2. Customers—Psychology. 3. Color—
        Psychological aspects. I. Title.

        HF5438.8.P75B63 2006   658.8'342   C2006-902284-4.

Design assistance: David Macpherson
Layout & typeset by: Ingénieuse Productions, Edmonton, AB
Printed and Bound in the United States of America

Contents

It is unlikely that there is anyone in the world who can make you work harder. That is something which only your self-motivation can accomplish. But along with that come the tools of working smarter and of having more success with what you're currently doing.

Even if you didn't see any more more clients, what would it be like if you were able to be more successful with your current efforts? You will still be way ahead of the game when you understand and use the power of Colors for yourself and your clients who communicate, buy, listen, value and stay loyal for very different reasons.

If you have already attended the Colors seminar, by now you've gone through a long list of sales you should have closed or can re-contact with the knowledge you now have about yourself and your clients. However, if you're reading this book, remember that the power of understanding our different personality types cannot come alive through this book alone. It is comparable to reading a travel guide in lieu of actually making the trip. Both are valuable, but reading about something is quite different than living the trip – or in this case, the practicality and powerful insights of the training. If you haven't attended the seminar, do whatever it takes to participate in one because it brings the tools and insights of Colors alive in practical and three-dimensional ways that no amount of reading can replace.

What's more important? Product knowledge, or an understanding of clients, their personality, motivators, ways of making decisions and values? There is no right or wrong answer, as both are invaluable. You've got to know your stuff— but you also have to know who you're stuffing! What do different personalities want from you and what do they look for or avoid? While each is unique, having an in-depth knowledge of Colors can make a difference in your success, presentation of information, and some definite tools to know what to avoid. Discovering a client's Colors, ways of communicating and purchase preferences is NOT after your meeting is over.

All education, seminars or training are valuable to give you tips, insights, and product knowledge. They are like a road map with all the details, but they don't do the driving for you. It is still up to you to do the Colors seminar training, to use these tools and to incorporate some changes in your outlook and approach. Just waiting for things to happen is not a recipe for success. It will, more often than not, result only in regrets and wishes of should've and could've.

The first challenges are two things to stop doing: Saying: '*I'll try*' out loud and '*I can't*' to yourself. '*I can't*' just keeps reminding yourself of your limitations, the vast majority of which are self-imposed and not true at all.

Are you prepared to step out of your comfort zone? After all, it's not called a comfort zone because it's comfortable. It's called that because it's uncomfortable for your personality type to step out of it. But your growth, strengthening the relationships with your clients, successfulness and many other things that may be just out of your comfort zone. With your fears and faith that you can do it, can you step out of it? Can you choose to spend the same time and energy telling yourself that of course '*you can do it*' and to make the effort of looking at things through slightly different glasses? When you say you will try, more often than not it is to hide your belief of feeling that you cannot do something, that you don't want to say no, or tell someone to get off your case when you have no intention of doing it at all. It is always fine to say you will make your best efforts, just avoid the phrase '*I'll try*'.

Keep growing and learning the power of Colors. It's worth it and you're worth it.

George J. Boelcke, F.C.I.

Until the pain of where you are is bigger than the perceived pain of where you need to go, you won't move.

Each year companies spend thousands of dollars on advertising and marketing in an effort to attract new clients. After all, without customers, there isn't much of a business, is there? From radio to print media, and billboards to flyers, vastly different approaches are used in an effort to connect with potential customers and to attract them to deal with us. Not too many years ago, the typical marketing campaign revolved around particular age groups. Anyone who wanted to attract affluent buyers between 45 and 64 might advertise on 60 Minutes, for example.

These days however, much more effective marketing is geared towards personality types. Attracting groups who live for fun and adventure on the weekends, have a lot of disposable income and like to buy the latest and greatest is the equivalent of marketing to high Orange people. Sears is another excellent example of effectively targeting personality types through programs such as Extreme Home Makeover. A great feel-good show which connects in powerful ways with vast numbers of high Blues, who are attracted to the show for so many reasons.

A company like General Motors figured out years ago, that Golds are the largest group in the country, and started using the song "Like A Rock" as part of their advertising. In fact, they've used it for more than one hundred commercials over the years. Why? Because it works as a strong appeal to Golds. What does the phrase "Like a Rock" state or imply? Stable, count on me, not going to let you down, reliable, solid, dependable and many other adjectives that can quickly come to mind when a high Gold hears that phrase. It really does describe them very well.

Yet in that same business, why do car dealers, many of whom have been in business for decades, need to keep spending tens of thousands of dollars on advertising each month? Yes, anytime you see a color full-page newspaper ad, you know they've spent a huge amount of money. After all those years in business, shouldn't there be very little advertising and a ton of repeat business?

Yes there should – but there isn't. It's almost as though dealerships choose to work hard, instead of also working smart, through understanding the needs and stresses of their customers. To my knowledge, there isn't a single dealership which has ever participated in an effective Colors seminar to get the powerful insights into their customers and to simply learn to do more of what works and less of what quickly turns off clients from ever coming back. Not to mention that the vast majority of owners are high Gold, set in their ways and unwilling to invest in training of almost any kind.

On top of that, dealerships continue to have turnover in sales staff ranging between 50 and 100 percent a year on average. So when Green has established the credibility of a sales person and they leave – they'll start from scratch – and usually somewhere else. Blues care most about connecting with the person. They don't buy from the dealer, they buy from, and stay loyal to, the sales person who is long gone. Plus Golds look for someone who keeps their word, honors their commitment and provides service after the sale. It is a sure-fire way to get Golds off the price issue and focused on service. Right there, 80 percent of repeat business is tuned out and turned off when their sales person is gone.

Does an understanding of Colors matter to you or your company? It matters a lot if you chose to work smarter, work better as a team and understand that it's not about how you sell, but rather about what your customers want and value. This is both the greatest challenge and opportunity for you and your success. Or in the words of a Wharton University ad:

Good news:	20% of your customers generate 150% of your profits
Bad news:	You don't know who they are
Worse news:	You regularly tick them off

Getting to Yes

Most customers really want to say yes and to stop shopping around. Almost all have an inner need and drive to get something done, implemented or purchased. You just need to make it possible by getting them to feel secure, relaxed, and confident they have picked the right place and the right person.

For each Color, this involves different steps and sales approaches. None are designed to make you phony, but rather to get out of your Color and connect in meaningful ways to honor customers in ways in which they wish to be dealt with. You won't close every customer, but a small change in your approach can have a big payoff. After all, preparation breeds confidence. Plus if you lose the sale, don't lose the lesson.

Love the company, or hate it, everyone knows that Wal-Mart is the world's largest retailer. But their success really happens behind the scenes with their sophisticated computer software, tracking ability, attention to details, discipline and an environment where everyone understands that knowledge really is power.

When it comes to their customers, Wal-Mart also leaves nothing to chance in an effort to maximize profits, store visits, customer service and retention. It is the reason that it came as no surprise when a Wal-Mart Vice President recently shared the insight that Wal-Mart knows that a lost customer costs the company $215,000. We don't know what's included in that figure, or how much influence a lost customer has over others, but we can be sure that Wal-Mart has the figure accurate and knows (not guesses or wonder) what a lost or turned-off customer costs them.

For you, this is exactly the same. Whether it's a lost customer or one you simply didn't get, there is always a cost involved. You may not have a concrete dollar figure, but you cannot grow when you don't gain new business, nor when you're spending a large part of your efforts in simply replacing your clients.

But it all starts with an understanding of yourself and the strengths and stresses of your Colors. After all, if you don't know yourself— losing a client is an expensive way to find out and experiment with.

- Customers will deal with you if they trust you. Credibility is huge, although different for all Colors.

- Most Color groups seldom change their mind after saying no.

- Create an understanding that sometimes cheap actually costs more and build value.

- Voice inflection changes everything.

- Customers quickly forget the price but remember the service and the quality— complaints are almost never over money issues.

- Under promise and over deliver— keep your word and honor your commitments.

- Get out of jargons and shortcuts— customers have never heard your industry buzzwords. Are you giving them inside information and educating them, or talking down to them and making them feel stupid? It happens easily and some Colors are very sensitive to catching this, but will never tell you.

- Cross selling involves relationships and a level of trust— only then will customers let you focus on convenience, cost saving and other factors. Until you are in the door you cannot take the next step.

- Your choice of words make a big difference— cost vs. investment, pay us vs. invest in your... Are you helping them to go broke or invest in themselves?

Strengths of Colors in Sales

The Blue Person:

- good at relationship selling and multi-tasking
- customer oriented— open and friendly
- creative ideas and problem-solving solutions
- easily connects in caring ways
- intuitive in meeting the customers' needs
- excels at listening and verbal skills
- enjoys the challenge of selling IF they believe in the product or service
- aware of organizational climate and their teammates

The Gold Person:

- will provide details, options and concrete advice
- first focus in sales is on firms' strengths and reputation over the specific product or service
- will achieve goals which they have committed to
- excels at getting the sale and all details, can be impatient when delayed
- greatly values the company image, reputation, chain of command, policies, and stability
- practical, direct, efficient and to-the-point
- values and promotes a bottom line approach
- on-time and organized. Reports, stats, notes, and orders are completed when required

The Green Person:

- enjoys marketing new, latest, and innovative products and services
- focus on big picture sale, implication and integration
- excellent technical and product knowledge
- excels at teaching others— staff and clients
- product oriented— how it will fit in with larger issues
- factual and logical— non-emotional selling
- will have a thorough knowledge and answers to all possibilities before starting
- provides well thought-out feedback on improvements or growth challenges

The Orange Person:

- excellent hands-on problem solver if issues arise
- loves variety of products and options
- great at selling what can be negotiated
- motivator of team and clients, lateral thinker
- thrives on winning the sale or contest
- looks for new challenges in products/services and problems to solve
- looks for short-term contests and bonus plans
- self motivated to succeed 'their way'

When it comes to sales,
Blues are farmers and Orange are hunters.

- presentations need logic, specifics and all the details. Stay on track and get to the point

- honor their time— don't be late or stay past the length of the appointment

- professional (neat) dress, attitude and demeanor

- results oriented— communicate in clear and concise manner

- stay value conscious and bottom-line focused

- be aware of their strong desire to finish what they start— buying decisions included. They will give you feedback and a decision deadline which will be adhered to

- remain formal and business-like. Do not get over-friendly or make small-talk beyond basic business polite

- target and focus on specifics, results, practical aspects and details

- get commitment of how much time they've allocated for your meeting and stick to it

- recognize their awards, certificates and achievements on the wall

- high fear factor of making the wrong decision

- very loyal to current company— tried and true approach— *'we always...'* type of comments and approach

- they are creatures of habit, be aware of their challenge with changes and doing something different without solid reasons

- never over-promise, get carried away, or become too optimistic as almost everything is evaluated against their own practicality scale

- sales or explanations in a step-by-step fashion keeping a focus on the practical aspects

- take the time to cover the strengths and history of the company to build credibility with them

- realistic goals and practical steps on achieving them since too much (almost any) dreaming or *'unrealistic'* goals will quickly have them tuned out

- they want to make the right decision with all the information and details in a timely manner. It is very unlikely they will change their minds later

- connect to what they are currently doing or practicing and use the words upgrade or improve— not the word change

- if you're late— you're dead. Call ahead (or greet them) and give them the option of still meeting or re-scheduling— they are on-task and have lots on their to-do list

- give them choices— nothing overwhelming, or too many, but be cognizant that they want to make their own decisions and hate to be told something has to be done, or can only be done one way

- they have a small but *real* circle of friends and are very private, so referrals from this group will be hard to obtain. It also means you will need to explain why you are requesting anything but basic personal information from them

- don't drop by— ever. They value their organization and schedule and insist you call ahead and make an appointment

- praise their conservative approach, ability to spend money wisely, efficiency, and detailed nature

- supply written back-up material, brochures or written presentation. They look for material to review after your meeting so make sure it is well organized and professional

- assure them that your product or service has longevity and staying power to make sure they won't have to revisit the issue again in the near future

"You guys are late! You're providing a service to us, yet you kept us waiting? In a normal business you wouldn't even get in the front door!"
Gold CEO to a
Donald Trump Apprentice team

What You Tend to
See and Hear From Gold

- stays on track and focused
- looks at watch frequently
- only basic small-talk
- prefers written presentation
- serious demeanor
- frequent either-or phrases
- always gets back on track
- won't share personal stories
- business-like manner
- keeps hands under control
- can have neutral expression
- wants it in writing and proven
- closed-ended questions
- talks and asks about specifics
- controlled
- reserved and private
- wants and asks about all the details
- looks for written material
- talks in point form
- dressed more formal and neat
- note taker and list maker
- concerned demeanor
- focuses on the practical aspects
- starts and finishes on time
- often sounds stressed or words clipped and short
- suspect of new ideas
- even voice tone
- seeks (and is impatient for) closure
- short and direct answers
- talks of schedules/deadlines

For most Golds, buying decisions follow specific procedures and their own personal set of rules. It will be the ever-present juggling of finding the best value along with a good quality product or service. This scale applies to their life as well as purchases for their company.

The starting point will be the current tried, tested, and proven label, or a company that they are comfortable with, providing a stable track record and excellent customer service. They have always dealt there and will be reluctant to experiment or change to another company unless there are clear savings, or a better product. For that, they will need evidence. Preferably in writing with all the details, and wording that talks about superior or improved, instead of change.

Because of their loyalty, it does mean current suppliers, or companies, will likely have a chance to match the quote from someone else. It is the old Cold-War saying of *'trust but verify.'* It gives Golds the best of both worlds in getting the most value, while possibly avoiding the perceived dangers of changing companies.

Research on price and quality will be done in a methodical and systematic manner. This purchase has now made their to-do list. The focus is now on accomplishing the mission of getting it off this list as soon as possible. Delays of information or quotes will quickly frustrate them and have them showing their impatience. Obviously it is a group highly sensitive to wasting time and others not keeping their promises. It can easily be a reason they will abandon their current company to expedite the matter. They are very cognizant of bad service, unprofessional staff, or getting the run-around. But it is based only on their scale and perception.

Sometimes sales training explains that mistakes can happen, but the crucial issue is how the matter resolves itself. That is absolutely the case for Gold customers. The professionalism with which a mistake is owned up to and corrected is one of THE most important ways to retain the loyal Gold client. They are fully aware mistakes do happen, but the method in which it is addressed goes a very long way to building their loyalty. On the other hand, if they have been mistreated, have not had their concerns addressed, been given excuses, or quotes and information is not supplied when needed, this company will be off their 'list' immediately with little chance of future business. It would just be a waste of time to go there again in the future, will be their fixed mindset.

Also factored in is their high sensitivity to making mistakes of any kind. They are conservative and traditional by nature, very responsible, and excellent with money. Even with company funds, their mindset considers it *their* money and won't be wasted. After all, it is their butt if the smallest thing goes wrong. That will have big repercussions (in their view), plus likely makes them look incompetent. All things to avoid at any cost.

"The only guarantee I make
is that I'll follow through
on a commitment I've made."
Greg Norman

- start with overview before getting to the necessary specifics

- stress latest, greatest, efficiencies and technologically advanced

- do not rush or push for closure or decision— the more pressure, the less likely you are to get the sale. You are a supplier of information for them. Nothing more— nothing less

- do not look for emotional reactions or friendly chit-chat, they are not interested in becoming your friend

- stick to the facts

- do not interrupt when they are thinking something through. Yes, there can be frequent moments of silence while they process and evaluate your comments

- stay patient and draw out their questions, goals and ideas

- allow them input into the why, how, integration or custom changes

- evidence, facts, and proof— never your opinion, hype or pitch

- get the little agreements first before moving on. Do not over-sell or over-talk

- stay factual and logical without emotional appeals or strong sales tactics

- remember their need for credibility— build that into your presentation, way of explaining, material, proposals, handouts and everywhere else

- when communicating by email or letter they look for credibility through spelling an grammatical mistakes— it is all they can look at, so proofread it before pressing the send button

- be prepared for many specific and probing questions at your follow-up meetings, and to supply extra technical information others would not ask for

- do not pressure for the close. Trial questions are fine, but be mindful that if you push for an answer it will often be 'no' and that may be almost impossible to move them from later

- don't bluff. Remember they do their research and can know more about the subject than you do, but will often ask questions where they know the answer simply to test you. If you don't know, tell them you will find out and get back to them

- keep your promises and commitments— they rely on it. When possible, do it by e-mail

- small talk and excessive social situations make them uncomfortable— do not expose them to it unnecessarily. They will not banter back and forth

- avoid finishing their sentences, thoughts, or jumping in. They are people of few words, well chosen, and correctly worded

- their normal lack of facial expressions and passive communication methods are their style. Don't take it personally or look for visual signs of whether you are on-track or making progress

- don't give up— stay in touch and supply information they can learn from— especially if it is written or available to them on the web

- once they understand the concept and have researched the material on their own time, they will have lots of questions— get ready, stay patient and assure you write them all down or address them

- don't waste your time making friendships. They know you are pitching something, and they're choosy about their friends

- don't bother name dropping— it is more of an insult than sales tool. What do they care if so-and-so *got taken*

- stay on track and focused without jumping around from subject to subject

- you only got the appointment because they see a need or a way to improve something. It was not your sales ability, so allow them to take control of the meeting/goals/process and agenda

What do you want badly enough that you're prepared to step out of your comfort zone for?

What You Tend to
See and Hear From Green

- neutral demeanor
- wants brochures and material
- can make you feel judged
- wants details and fine print
- skeptical attitude
- formal and reserved
- very sure of themselves
- asks credibility questions
- seldom correct themselves
- can look up when thinking
- will not show emotions (of any kind) easily
- clothes (what to wear) not that important
- slight delay in responding
- few words— well chosen
- well informed and knowledgeable
- technical and why or how questions
- dry sense of humor and sarcasm
- will respond when they're ready
- asks *weird* (why would that matter) questions
- poker face
- thinks things through (before deciding or answering)
- weighs decisions and answers
- serious and business-like
- tends to gesture from the head
- passive listener
- probing questions
- large vocabulary
- not overly friendly
- brief and concise
- no small talk or buddy-buddy approach

All in all, Greens would rather reinvent the outdated and inefficient sales and buying process. It takes time to drive somewhere, get into the store, then hope they even have the product in a variety of different styles and options, not to mention dodging annoying sales staff, and certainly never having enough time to explore their choices and options. Plus there is the likelihood of being forced to interact with staff that are too talkative and appear to have been hired yesterday, based on their lack of in-depth knowledge. But until then, chatty staff will get a curt answer and a definite signal of *'leave me alone.'* After all, their buying trips are more of an investigation than a shopping trip.

Sales staff are really only useful to give them information. Even then, it is taken with a grain of salt as these people are promoting their own product and really have no credibility in the eyes of a Green investigator— ah— purchaser. If sales staff choose not to leave them alone, any Green will simply leave the store to get away as soon as possible. If Greens are allowed their space, they will immediately start playing with the product, testing features, confirming options, pushing buttons and checking the manuals. There is no reason for a hasty decision. After all, they've already researched the product on the internet. This trip is to physically see and touch— and perhaps buy if everything they've learned already can be confirmed. Loose ends, questions, or something incompatible will certainly have them walk out of the store empty handed.

Once all available information has been gathered or confirmed, Green will narrow the field to a couple of models. At this point, a sales person might actually be of some use. Unfortunately, Greens can't help themselves. One or two of the first questions can be technical, and such where they already know the answer. However, in their effort to establish credibility, they're simply seeking to test that of the sales person. Part of this interrogation is to confirm his or her hypothesis, part is making sure there are no flaws or limitations that may have been overlooked. After that, Green takes the time to process all available information and forms a logical conclusion. Mission accomplished— case closed. Then, of course, comes the long journey of making the product function in the real world and real-life experimenting and testing. Oh, and making sure they do check the web for any further information as long as there's an opportunity to return it if something better appears to be released soon.

Throughout, the Green has handled the sales process in a logical fashion. They require access to information, web sources, a database, and a knowledgeable expert to fill in the details and confirm information. No pitch, buddy-buddy tactics, or smooth talking has any impact on their mission or decision. Few things irritate them more than any sales person, who is obviously commission-driven, and skewing their data with biased information. Plus they will want to chit-chat to become their best friend— no thanks.

"I'm gonna take a little time—
a little time to think things over."
Foreigner

- don't tell them— ask and involve them instead

- stay upbeat and optimistic. Roll with the punches and know they firmly believe that they can do anything

- frequent interrupter and finishes other people's sentences

- attention getting activities

- likes cool gifts and neat gadgets

- let them take control of the overall how questions once they understand where you are going. It allows them to contribute to the sale and make their own decisions on implementation, methods and process

- be ready for direct and blunt feedback and questions. They will tell it like it is. It is not an insult— it's just their style

- as name-droppers, it wouldn't hurt if you had references of big names or a cool story of someone well known

- asking you to leave written material is a clue they want you out and likely won't actually read it

- give them an overview and outline first. They will ask if they want more details

- keep your energy level up, show a sense of humor, and verbal affirmations

- don't get hung up on specifics. Keep explanations to the length of time it takes for an elevator ride

- be mindful of their great filter of information: Is it practical, can I use it right now, will it make me money, what's in it for me, or is it fun and quick?

- stay out of your judgments when they show their multi-tasking skills, get interrupted or start doing other things at the same time as your meeting

- avoid excessive paperwork, it is a very big turn-off and a quick way to lose them. Assure them that most of the paperwork is yours to do and not theirs

- be flexible, throw away your agenda and formal presentation plans. You will not be in control and might as well embrace it

- conversations, questions, and presentations will get off track and jump from point to point very quickly— be ready and stay flexible

- get to the point— don't bore them

- realize that they may pull others into the meeting to get feedback and expedite the decision making process or catch details they may miss

- be ready to start again as they may well assign this to someone else

- they function through hunches and make quick decisions. Do not oversell

- ask for the business and make it painless, quick and fun. They have many other things on the go, so make sure you have a fast-forward method where appropriate, or when you see them start to tune you out and start to focus on other things

Orange Sales Tools

- if they trust you— they will buy and let you *'take care of it'* from start to finish— but you had better come through

- it is possible to see them without an appointment if you have a good reason. Bring a cool gift or make sure you don't abuse their need for quick meetings

- missing an appointment with you is not always a sign they aren't interested at all. There's so much happening they may forget or delay you for something more important

- give them a deal. They value winning and a deal or discount makes it a win for them. But they won't have the patience or time to get to the bottom-line price because speed also matters

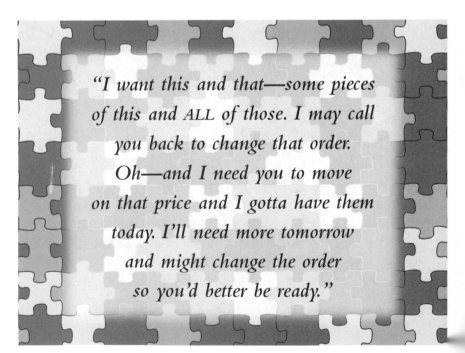

"I want this and that—some pieces of this and ALL of those. I may call you back to change that order. Oh—and I need you to move on that price and I gotta have them today. I'll need more tomorrow and might change the order so you'd better be ready."

What You Tend to
See and Hear From Orange

- attention getting activities
- anything's possible outlook— very optimistic
- multi-tasking all the time
- laughter/stories/playful nature
- agreeable and a can-do attitude
- demonstrates extreme confidence
- direct comments and feedback
- trendy/fashionable dresser
- sports stuff lying around
- fun/happy and always 'on'
- fast paced, direct and to the point
- frequent use of hands
- quick answers and/or decisions
- finishes others' sentences
- dramatic and flamboyant
- sense of humor
- excited, active and fidgety
- can embellish stuff and stories
- wants the last word
- unfinished sentences
- wants to speed things up and shortcut
- messy office
- frequent interruptions
- latest/greatest/cool stuff
- no need for appointment— come on in
- animated expressions
- spontaneous and impatient
- active and moving around
- name-dropper
- designer labels

While this is a group that has few fixed rules, one of them is definitely to get the buying done— NOW! Actual shopping will be a hit and go method with a firm belief that if they haven't found what they're looking for after one or two stores— they're done. It was not that important and they'll deal with it another day. Right now there are other things to do that are a lot more fun than being stuck in a mall and having all their life and energy sucked out of them.

Important factors for Orange are the speed to get it bought, the convenience, and a definite cool factor. This is especially true for their personal purchases. They love the latest, greatest, and trendiest— all of which contribute to assuring others notice. Purchases for their company will generally be passed to someone else and avoided, if at all possible. It is just too much of a hassle, and most sales staff give them an overload of information or details— none of which an Orange needs to make a decision. Anyone who starts with manufacturing specs and a large catalogue will be quickly shut down. At that point, Orange will gladly ask to have the material left to review. It won't happen, of course. It will be passed to someone else, or forgotten and buried. It is simply the get-away package to have the sales person out of the office as soon as possible.

When they do have to make purchases, one of the first places to start looking is via the telephone. It will involve calls to their large circle of contacts. After all, this is the greatest networking group of all Colors. Someone will know who to call that can get this handled.

Of course, they value a sales person that can show up quickly, stay flexible and give them a high energy, brief overview without too many details. Yes, it would help that it's the same stuff Donald Trump has in his office, as that would go a long way to gaining their interest. Up-selling them at this point can be done without much difficulty if there are other things Orange needs to purchase at the same time. After all, while you're there, maybe we can just get these other things handled and out of my hair, too. Once they have found a person they're comfortable with, and who will make things quick and smooth, let's get it over with right now— can often be their attitude.

In the perfect world, Orange wants it quick and convenient, fun, and cool. It is not a matter of money. Few things are measured by their cost, but rather whether something is worth having. When that's established, money is not one of the main factors. They need it, they buy it. Even the purchase of their last vehicle took less than a couple of hours for the vast majority of Orange. So why would any smaller purchase need to be dragged out forever?

"You gotta have fun no matter what you do! If your joy button has been permanently removed, you're gonna have real difficulties."
Charles Adler,
Corus Radio Talk Show host

- they value and look for caring, empathy and a very soft spoken approach

- talk about people, their team, and common goals

- too many facts, figures, and written material will turn them off in a hurry

- point out the features and benefits of your product or service as it will positively impact their team and others

- presentations need to stay fun, stimulating, and allow adequate time for socializing

- retain personal exchanges and relationship building. Until you have established a relationship with them, you cannot have a sale

- big picture people, not overly detail-oriented. If you need follow through on details— get them in writing

- stay personal, asking open-ended questions and really listen to their answers and feedback

- always look for their input, opinions, and feelings expressed

- support and encourage them to share their dreams or goals as it might fit in with your product or service

- be mindful that they cannot come out and say 'no'. That means you will likely not get a direct answer if they have tuned out

- short answers from them are a very good clue that something is wrong, but they're not comfortable giving you direct feedback

- a good rule of thumb is that at least a third of your time needs to be spent on building the relationship before you can ever hope to connect with them

- dream with them about the future, possibilities, doing it better and/or making a difference

- this is your largest group of referrals once they feel you care about them more than the sale

- their strong sense of intuition means they can spot a phony a mile away. Be yourself, do not attempt to become Blue— it will not work. Build the relationship in your own (Color) and personal way, but make sure you do show genuine interest in them, their family, and (almost always) their pets

- make sure they understand feedback will not affect your relationship. They do not want to make waves or supply negative information or comments

- take whatever time you thought would be needed and double it. This allows time for sharing and avoids making them feel pressured or rushed for any reason

- stop looking at your watch, over their shoulder and sending many other non-verbal signals that Blues are very aware of

- don't look for logical explanations. Things will feel right for them even if they are not totally able to explain why as they function in-esteem when they follow their strong sense of intuition

- you cannot attack the competition— they do not respond to negative sales attempts as they do have a relationship with someone else— somewhere

- an appointment is not always necessary as they may be glad to see you again. People are always more important than paperwork

- invest the time and effort in a thank you card. Doing something nice and thoughtful is a way for them to measure whether you really care

- if others need help, they can run late for your meeting. Do not show your impatience or annoyance as they'll easily pick up on your non-verbal clues

- be prepared to sell their team when others are often pulled in to make group decisions.

- avoid overly technical presentations or sales talks. It's not that they wouldn't understand, it's just that they don't care that much about it

"Hello, retailers. Let me introduce myself. I'm a Relational Shopper. I'm not looking for bargains or the lowest price in town. I'm looking for a retailer I can trust. One I can feel comfortable buying from again and again. It could be the beginning of a lasting relationship" Corus Radio Calgary Ad

What You Tend to
See and Hear From Blue

- frequent use of humor
- open-ended questions
- feelings shown and expressed
- positive spin on everything
- gives and seeks longer answers
- warm and huggable clothing
- animated expressions
- warm and very friendly demeanor
- pulls others into conversations
- unselfish and almost always accommodating
- can sugarcoat comments, feedback and answer
- checks before interrupting
- stops paperwork for anyone
- looks to personal discussion
- avoids conflicts or negatives
- talks with their hands
- open body position
- story teller
- frequent use of touch
- dreams and possibilities
- leans forward to listen
- soft and soothing voice
- says sorry a lot
- visible emotions
- listen attentively
- polite manner
- can gesture from the heart
- 'I feel' sentences
- relationship building words and demeanor
- very agreeable

A high Blue interior decorator regularly purchases over $50,000 for the content of show homes. With her list in hand, she chats up, and almost interviews, sales staff in a large furniture store. Her drive and mission is to find a single mom, or other sales person, who clearly needs the commission before she simply hands over the list. When she has found this person, she couldn't be happier. The shopping is done and she has accomplished a very big self-esteem builder in helping someone deserving at the same time.

For most high Blue, buying happens first through building a relationship. Any salesperson calling on a high Blue needs to be very aware of this. They will want to get to know the person first before jumping into the business part.

Blue needs to make a connection, which will become a strong bond to give them a reason to deal with that person. Price is definitely not one of the most important issues they consider once they trust the person they're dealing with. They value the personal touch of an office visit and being able to deal with someone face to face as a person, instead of a phone order, in most cases.

Because decisions should be made as a team, it will often involve others being pulled into a sales presentation. That allows the Blue to get the input from others and to reach a consensus. It is their team-player way to operate and also avoids sticking their neck out to make the decision on their own. This way, they do not risk alienating their team members, or possibly being second-guessed after the fact.

It makes it a bit of a challenge to actually know who the purchaser is during any meeting. The Blue person may be the quarterback, but will not be the most vocal person in asking questions, probing, or challenging answers and forcing comparisons to another company. Their choice of who to deal with, or product to purchase, may well be overridden. Others with stronger opinions, or those who are more vocal, may well win the day. The other challenge is their desire to fit in and to be accommodating. It means they will seldom come right out and say no, or let anyone know they're going to deal somewhere else.

When it comes to personal shopping, this will often be a social event. It tends to be an outing, to be enjoyed in the company of friends and family. It can frequently include lunch, a drink, or dinner afterwards. If possible, it will be done as a group that enjoys wandering through the mall where chatting and sharing stories is just as important as the buying part of the trip.

When I close my eyes I see —
the way this world shall be.
Garth Brooks

What to Look For

In addition to the list of 30 general clues to each Color, just watching people will give you many clear signals. Frequently looking at their watch is a good clue of a high Gold person. After all, they value staying on time. So looking at their watch or just having a big clock in their office, is one of the general signs for Gold since it acts as their compass. It will not tell you their Color, but it is another piece of the puzzle in looking to their behavior, words, dress, action, and demeanor.

It is important to remember that these are general clues for each Color, and each was prefaced with the words: *What you tend to see and hear*. It is not meant as a list to check off. For example, a high Blue/Orange female in a male dominated corporate office, will often show many outward behaviors of Orange. This is a *'safer'* Color for her to draw because of her specific environment.

Some other clues and signals will include:

- How do they walk?
- What is their facial expression?
- Do they display a sense of humor?
- Is there physical touch?
- Which way do they respond to questions? Quickly and openly or hedging, reserved and thinking it through first?
- Are they on time, ready and prepared for you, or scrambling and running late?
- Are they active or passive listeners?
- How do they communicate— closed or welcoming and smiling at everyone?
- How do they put things in their briefcase, purse or wallet?
- How do they handle line-ups, waiting, delays or stress?

- What's on their desk— how neat is it?

- What kind of pictures are on their walls or fridge, if any? Family pictures, fun stuff or an organizer and calendar?

- Do they come across as open and welcoming or more business-like and closed?

- What do you hear from them? Words about feelings or logic— being information from their heart or their head?

- What are the words? Business-like and point form, few words, warm and caring or fast and animated?

- What about their general demeanor? Concerned or skeptical, welcoming and inclusive or relaxed, flexible and fun?

BUT: When you are seeing or hearing these clues, are you staying out of your judgments? Are you seeing the actual behavior at face value? Or are you putting your interpretation and spin on it? Are you using your scale and fixed Color beliefs to judge the 93 percent non-verbal communication, or just factually and without filtering, observing it? There is a BIG difference.

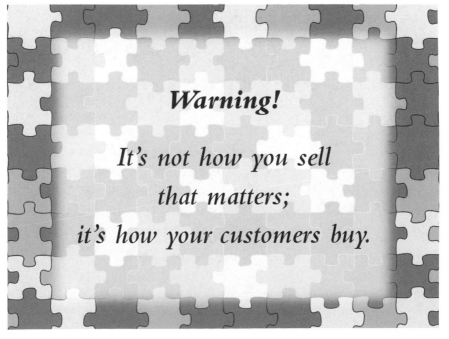

Warning!

It's not how you sell
that matters;
it's how your customers buy.

When in Doubt – Ask!

There are also easy questions to ask in an effort to get more clues as to their Colors. You ask many of them now, but perhaps do not evaluate the answer in terms of gaining an insight into the other persons' Colors. Each answer will get you closer to being able to honor and value them by speaking 'their language,' in their Color.

For example: A Gold will specifically tell you that he or she has 15 minutes, where a Blue will not commit to such a tight time-frame. A Gold or Green will always have you make an appointment so they can stay pro-active, be prepared, and plan, while most Blue or Orange will not want to be tied down to a specific time, but only a range.

In the same way, Gold and Green will tend to make their appointments well in advance, while Blue and Orange will see you much more quickly if they're interested.

...Should we make an appointment or would you like me to drop by this afternoon?
(Blue and Orange are almost always flexible in this area as people are not an interruption, but frequently a welcome break from paperwork)

...Would you like me to walk you through the details and specifics or an overview of the big picture first?
(Gold and Green do want all the details. Orange and Blue may ask, but it is often unlikely)

...Would you prefer I e-mail/mail the information to you or would you like to go through it with me in person?

...*Should I start going through the effects and benefits for your staff first, or the product/material/service aspects?*
(The impact on people is an important primary consideration for Blues)

...*What do you like best about your current supplier/rep or company?*
(focus on people, long-time/always dealt there, etc.)

...*What challenges do you have with them now?*
(credibility, won't keep their word, can't keep up, etc.)

...*Do you need the information (would you prefer the information) before we discuss it?*
(i.e.: e-mail or fax in advance)

...*How much time do you have to walk through this?*

...*Price/cost aside, what do you value/look for?*
(people things, efficiency, accommodate last minute scrambling, improved process or product, etc.)

...*Would you like the material in writing?*
(brochure, presentation, etc.)

The common denominator in almost every corporation is Gold. From structure to scheduling, from paperwork to accountability, almost every company functions as a Gold environment.

So when in doubt, it is always safe to start on the assumption you are also communicating with a Gold person until you hear and see different clues as to their color. Communicate with others on their terms. It is not a matter of being a phony but honoring others in terms they can understand and value.

How Do You Set Your Goals?

In sales, or other areas of life, should goals always be reached, or at least be realistically achievable? Or is it OK to set the bar quite high and make your best efforts to get close? The answer will give you a huge clue as to someone's Colors. The former certainly applies to Golds, while any self-respecting Orange will shoot for the moon and coming close always counts. In fact, high Oranges will generally admit that reaching their goals actually means they were set too low in the first place.

It will show very clearly with a simple question: Would you rather set an income goal of $100k and get to $80k, or a goal of $60k and achieve it? Almost every Gold will choose the realistic $60k goal. After all, few things are more important to Golds, and few things matter more when they decide to deal with you or become friends, than keeping their word. Yet almost every high Orange will pick the goal of $100k and the possibility of falling short. Why? "We want to keep pushing ourselves, the higher the goal, the better, anyone can do $60k," and more feedback along those lines.

So what's better? A goal that you can take to the bank, or a seemingly impossible goal, but reaching most of it? If it sounds silly, you don't understand the mindset of a high Gold. But then, the question shouldn't be what's better. It should be: what's more satisfying, what creates less stress, what makes you feel like a winner, or how do you think others will judge you if you don't achieve your goal.

The Eyes Have It

Along with physical touch such as a hand on your shoulder, Blues have a strong need to look someone in the eyes. It must have been a Blue who coined the saying that the eyes are the window to the soul.

What a shame most sales staff are not familiar with Colors and this powerful and important lesson. After all, Blues are some of the most loyal clients, as well as a great source of referrals. But to deal with them should almost always start in person and not by telephone or e-mail.

It is the same reason high Blues are really uncomfortable talking with their backs to someone— anyone. They value making eye contact, to see your expression, to better connect with you and the chance to use their huge sense of intuition. But almost all of these require face to face communication. In any sales situation, find a way to meet your Blue clients in person. It'll be well worth the time.

Do It Now

Create a sense of urgency. It eliminates distractions, helps you focus and stay with what needs to be done. It is also a huge way for others you work with to see how to become successful, and your genuine urgency makes customers move. It is also way out of the comfort zone for every Color but Orange. Part of that is not to have an appointment unless you have someplace else to be afterwards. Never go on an appointment unless you have another appointment— even if your next meeting is to see your partner or to pick up your kids. It is a sure-fire way to keep you focused, it takes the fluff out of your meetings and gives you a legitimate reason to get on with it, stay focused, ask for the business, and move!

Can we do it now, sooner, faster, shorter? If your attitude is that your time is valuable, it will always leak into your talk, behavior, winning attitude and success.

People Come First

Results do not start with products or sales. They begin with service and people. Always have and always will. Results certainly matter, but relationships matter more and when relationships deteriorate, results will decline. You cannot build your client base or create loyal customers through e-mail or voicemail. In that same way, contentment, complacency and taking relationships for granted kills improvement and growth.

Relationships matter in all your interactions with team members, bosses, individual clients and any company you deal with. Think of a boss or company that you really enjoyed working for, and what factors mattered the most to you about the relationship? What about your favorite restaurant. What brings you back? Isn't it almost always the places with great service and staff who really care, seem to enjoy their jobs and make you feel welcome? Feeling valued is one of the most important factors in all of our purchase experiences and reasons for staying loyal, whatever the circumstances or situations.

Telling Them Apart

One of the more common questions is to be able to tell a high Blue from a high Orange. On the surface, both of these Colors can seem alike, as they both value people over paperwork or structure, have a very positive outlook, don't take themselves too seriously and share the view that life isn't measured by the clock. An easy way to tell the difference is through two ways:

Blues are much more patient. This ranges from longer meetings to not jumping into conversations. An easy outward sign is often through body movements. Orange will be much more likely to have something in their hands, doodle, get distracted, fidget, tap their feet or a host of other outward 'let's get going' signs. For Blues, this would be sign of disrespect and they're much more likely to listen patiently and attentively.

Orange also tends to say, or do things, which make them the center of attention, which includes the clothes they wear, jewelry, etc. Blues looking for attention do it in more subtle and less flashy ways.

Slow Down & Think Their Colors

Wow! I have to share this story with you because this Colors knowledge works in real ways. I'm very Orange and had a high Green client for over 15 months now. Her husband is Orange/Gold while she is quite Green. When I first started dealing with them, I sold them a $4 Million insurance policy. My Orange was able to close them quite quickly— although it was the husband's Orange that agreed when I suggested '*let's do it.*' Well the next day I received a call that they had changed their mind and were canceling.

A number of contacts after that did not get me any further forward on resurrecting the sale of the policy. Within the past couple of months I had pretty much given up on earning their business. I figured over a year of effort was quite enough. After all, my Orange impatience wanted to move on— with clients that I could actually close and see some results from.

Then I had the opportunity to do the Colors seminar and the light came on so clearly in looking back at so many customers. But particularly my Orange/Green client, who I hadn't talked to for a number of months. But a week after the seminar, I went at it again with my new tools and understanding.

I got close with the husband because of his high Orange '*let's get on with it*' approach that easily connected with me. Just like me, he was able to make the quick decision when he found the value. Now, however, I also very clearly realized that his high Green wife was absolutely not connecting with me. She was not comfortable at all with my Orange process, humor, speed and lack of detailed technical information.

Obviously she took some Green time, thought it through over night, and called in the morning to cancel the contract. I now understood, that in her eyes, she was totally un-comfortable with the process and lack of information. As a high Green she needed tons of detailed information, time to think, researched things on her own, and looked to making the perfect decision. Not to mention she looked for credibility in me which I wasn't showing by being so Orange around her. So it was a matter of taking a VERY deep breath, doubling the appointment time, developing credibility and getting out of my Orange behavior with her.

The appointment a week after the seminar and reading your book had me in a totally different mindset. Rather than pursuing the sale, I wanted to just go back to basics and build credibility that her high Green needed before ever proceeding. It wasn't going to be about my needs, mannerism or ways to do things, but about honoring her. It sure made sense when you said we speak four very different languages.

We went through a lot of information very thoroughly. Yes, her husband kept leaving— something like that is just too boring for a high Orange, don't I know that! She had certainly done her homework, which was easy to see based on her thorough and probing questions. Large parts of that were gaining more information for her, but I also knew that she was testing my credibility and seeing if I was going to be bluffing her, or giving correct answers. I did sense right away that now I was speaking her language and that something was very different in so many ways.

The $4 Million policy is done and a $350,000 mutual fund is being processed this week. Remember when we learned to do more of what works and less of what doesn't? Need I say more?

— R.W.

Order Form

#	Title	Investment per	Total amount
____	Colorful Personalities – Discover Your Personality Type Through the Power of Colors	Can $19.95 US $14.95	_____
____	Colorful Personalities – Audio CD	$9.95	_____
____	The Colors of Leadership & Mgmt.	$6.95	_____
____	The Colors of Parent & Child Dynamics	$6.95	_____
____	The Colors of Sales & Customers	$6.95	_____
____	The Colors of Relationships	$6.95	_____
____	¡Quédese con Su Dinero! Los Secretos del Crédito y la Deuda Lo que tiene que saber, lo que necesita evitar	$6.95	_____
____	It's Your Money! Tools, Tips and Tricks to Borrow Smarter and Pay It Off Quicker	US Edition: US $14.95 Can. Edition: CAD $19.95 Span. Edition: US $14.95	_____ _____ _____
	Tax & shipping (flat amount)		**$ 4.00**
	Total amount:		_____

Name: _____

Address: _____

City: _____ Pr./St.: _____ PC/Zip: _____

E-mail: _____

Payment enclosed by: ____check ____cash ____money order

Or Visa/MC: _____/_____/_____/_____ Exp date:___/__

Order by: Fax: (780) 432 5613 Web: www.yourmoneybook.com
E-mail: george@vantageseminars.com
Mail: Canada: Box 4080 Edmonton, AB, T6E 4S8
US: 1183-14781 Memorial Dr., Houston, TX 77079